Colours We Eat

Orange Foods

Patricia Whitehouse

www.raintreepublishers.co.uk
Visit our website to find out more information about **Raintree** books.

To order:

  Phone 44 (0) 1865 888112

  Send a fax to 44 (0) 1865 314091

🖳 Visit the Raintree Bookshop at **www.raintreepublishers.co.uk** to browse our catalogue and order online.

First published in Great Britain by Raintree,
Halley Court, Jordan Hill, Oxford OX2 8EJ,
part of Harcourt Education.
Raintree is a registered trademark of Harcourt
Education Ltd.

Editorial: Richard Woodham
Design: Richard Parker
Picture Research: Ruth Blair
Production: Jonathan Smith

Originated by Dot Gradations
Printed and bound in China by South China
Printing Company

ISBN 1 844 21448 6
08 07 06 05 04
10 9 8 7 6 5 4 3 2 1

British Library Cataloguing in Publication Data
Whitehouse, Patricia
Orange Foods
641.3
A full catalogue record for this book is available
from the British Library.

Acknowledgements
The publishers would like to thank the following
for permission to reproduce photographs:
Corbis pp. **4** (Ed Young), **6** (Paul A. Souders), **9**;
Dave Liebman p. **7**; Dwight Kuhn p. **14**;
GardenPhotos.com p. **15** (Judy White); Getty
Images pp. **10** (FoodPix), **13** (The Image Bank);
Heinemann Library pp. **5**, **8**, **11**, **12**, **16**, **17**, **18**,
19, **20**, **21**, **22**, **24** (Que-Net).

Cover photograph of an orange reproduced with
permission of Corbis.

Every effort has been made to contact copyright
holders of any material reproduced in this book.
Any omissions will be rectified in subsequent
printings if notice is given to the publishers.

CAUTION: Children should be supervised by an adult when handling food.

Some words are shown in bold, **like this.** You can find them in the glossary on page 23.

Contents

Have you eaten orange foods?

Colours are all around us.

How many different colours can you see in this picture?

All of these foods are orange.

Have you eaten any of them?

Which orange foods are big?

vine

Pumpkins are big and orange.

They grow on long **vines**.

squash

This squash is big and orange.

It grows on a long vine, too.

Which foods are orange inside?

pie

sweet potato

Sweet potatoes are orange on the inside.

They can be cooked in pies.

seed

This melon is orange on the inside.

It has many seeds inside. You cannot eat the seeds.

Which fruits are orange?

Apricots are small and orange.

They grow on trees.

peel

Tangerines are orange fruits.

The outside of a tangerine is called the **peel**.

Which orange foods are small?

These **lentils** are small and orange.

People cook lentils so they are soft enough to eat.

stone

Some nectarines are orange.

They have a big seed inside called a **stone**.

Which orange foods are crunchy?

Carrots are crunchy and orange.

The part we eat grows underground.

These peppers turn orange as they grow bigger.

They are used in crunchy salads.

Which orange foods are soft?

Some types of cheese are orange.

Cheese is made from milk.

peel

Marmalade is a soft spread.

Marmalade is made from orange **peels**.

Which drinks are orange?

You can drink orange juice.

People squeeze oranges to make orange juice.

mango

You can drink mango juice.

It is made from mangoes.

Recipe: Orange fruit salad

❗ Ask an adult to help you.

First, cut up some oranges, mangoes, melons, and tangerines.

Mix up the fruit pieces in a bowl.

Then, eat your orange salad!

Quiz

Can you name these orange foods?

Look for the answers on page 24.

Glossary

lentil
seed of a plant that you can cook and eat

marmalade
jam made from oranges

peel
skin of a fruit

stone
hard, central seed of many fruits

sweet potato
type of vegetable that grows underground

vine
plant that climbs around something as
it grows

Index

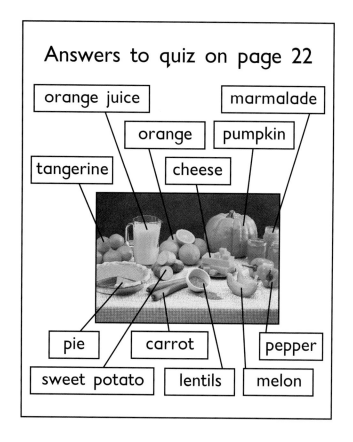

Answers to quiz on page 22

orange juice

marmalade

orange

pumpkin

tangerine

cheese

pie   carrot   pepper

sweet potato   lentils   melon

Titles in the Colours We Eat series include:

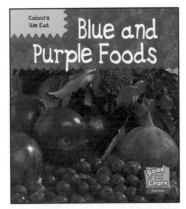

Hardback   184421446X

Hardback   1844214451

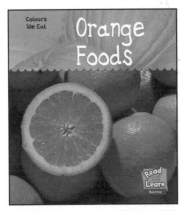

Hardback   1844214486

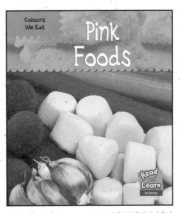

Hardback   1844214494

Hardback   1844214478

Find out about the other titles in this series on our website www.raintreepublishers.co.uk